1980

# The Road Again Taken

"  . . . Unlike the animals, [man] must construct his own behaviour from life and its experiences, and if set on this road of life, all will be well."
—MARIA MONTESSORI, in *Education for A New World.*

# The
# Road Again Taken

*Select Poems by*
Sheldon Christian

*Foreword by Prof.* RICHARD N. COFFIN

*Illustrations by* Thomas Bewick

The Pejepscot Press, Brunswick, Maine 04011

ACKNOWLEDGEMENT is hereby made to the editors and publishers of the following publications for permission to reprint here and hereafter the poems noted, first published in their pages: *America Speaking*, Altman Burns, editor, © 1942 by The Pirates Press, New York, for "I Know, Dear Heart"; *Christmas Lyrics of 1937*, © 1937 by Beacon Publications, New York, for "It Was Not Sleep"; *Granite Chips*, James Rinker, editor, copyright 1964 by The Poetry Society of New Hampshire, for "The Road Again Taken"; *The Maine Writers' Conference Chapbook*, Sheldon Christian, editor, for "Hi, Mabel," from No. 3; "The Nesters," from No. 4; "Snake Bite," from No. 5; "Boy Crossing A Field," from No. 6; "The Universal Tongue," from No. 7; "To Rebecca, Well Spiced," from No. 8; "Bumblebee," from No. 9; "Unto These Least," from No. 10; "Melanie" and "Ecology," from No. 11; "The Half-Bad Dog," "Celebration," and "Now," from No. 12; "If You'd Create" and "Elegy to A Lady Bug," from No. 13; "How Jason Found Paradise" and "Rip Van Wrinkles," from No. 14; "The Catbird and the Catalpa," "Condominium," and "Gentlemen Wear Jackets," from No. 15; "Mission Accomplished" and "Cana Revisited," from No. 16; and "Terminus" and "Ivy," from No. 17, copyright 1961, 1962, 1963, 1964, 1965, 1966, 1967, 1968, 1969, 1970, © 1972, 1973, 1974, and 1975, respectively, by The Pejepscot Press, Brunswick, Maine; *The Maine Writers' Conference Poetry Tournament* booklet for 1975, Adelbert M. Jakeman, Sr., editor, for "The Upward Reach"; *Motor Boating*, Walter R. Juettner, editor, Hearst Magazines, New York, for "The Changing Tide"; *Poetry of Today*, No. 30, 1934, a quarterly Supplement to *The Poetry Review* (London), for "Winter's Wind," here revised; *Portland* (Maine) *Evening Express*, December 12, 1963, for "J.F.K."; *Rock Ledge and Apple Blossoms*, an anthology, The Poetry Fellowship of Maine, 1971, for "View from the Window-Sill"; *The Specialty Salesman*, © 1964 by Specialty Salesman Magazine, Inc., for "Remember to Ask"; *The Tuftonian*, February, 1931, Sheldon Christian, editor, for "Athanasia"; *Unity* (Chicago), March 21, 1932, John Haynes Holmes, editor, for "Miracle"; and *The Wingèd Word*, Winter, 1943, copyright 1943 by Sheldon Christian, for "When, Seeing You Beside Me Fast Asleep."

# Contents

*Frontispiece* by Thomas Bewick . . . . . . . . . . . 2

FOREWORD . . . . . . . . . . . . . . . . 9

The Road Again Taken . . . . . . . . . . . . 11

The Pear Tree . . . . . . . . . . . . . . . 12

Bumblebee . . . . . . . . . . . . . . . . 13

Mission Accomplished . . . . . . . . . . . . . 14

Catbird in the Catalpa . . . . . . . . . . . . 15

In Perpetuum . . . . . . . . . . . . . . . . 16

The Sparrow Trap . . . . . . . . . . . . . . 17

The Trial of Goodwife Stover . . . . . . . . . . 18

Vapor Trail . . . . . . . . . . . . . . . . 20

What Happened at Fambridge Ferry . . . . . . . 21

Dr. Goss's Night Out . . . . . . . . . . . . . 22

Down East . . . . . . . . . . . . . . . . . 24

The Lying Soldier . . . . . . . . . . . . . . 25

Argentia-Bound . . . . . . . . . . . . . . . 26

The Changing Tide . . . . . . . . . . . . . . 27

A Good Day to Go to Church . . . . . . . . . . 28

The County Day of Prayer . . . . . . . . . . 29

The Doctor's Dictum . . . . . . . . . . . . . 30

Black Angel . . . . . . . . . . . . . . . . 31

5

The Fourth Dimension . . . . . . . . . . . . 32

Athanasia . . . . . . . . . . . . . . . 33

F/letcher's Progress . . . . . . . . . . . . . . 34

To Rebecca, Well Spiced . . . . . . . . . . . 35

When One Head Is Better Than Two . . . . . . . . 36

The Half-Bad Dog . . . . . . . . . . . . . . 37

Elegy to a Lady-Bug . . . . . . . . . . . . . . 38

View from the Window-Sill . . . . . . . . . . . 39

Remember to Ask . . . . . . . . . . . . . . 40

Snake Bite . . . . . . . . . . . . . . . . 41

Canine Rhapsody . . . . . . . . . . . . . . 42

The Sex Goddess . . . . . . . . . . . . . . 43

Boy Crossing A Field . . . . . . . . . . . . . 44

The Universal Tongue . . . . . . . . . . . . . 45

How Jason Found Paradise . . . . . . . . . . . 46

It Was Not Sleep . . . . . . . . . . . . . . 47

"Hi, Mabel!" . . . . . . . . . . . . . . . 48

The Nesters . . . . . . . . . . . . . . . . 49

Indian Summer . . . . . . . . . . . . . . . 50

Joe Weare, Indian Scout . . . . . . . . . . . . 51

Gentlemen Wear Jackets . . . . . . . . . . . . 54

Lady Debra . . . . . . . . . . . . . . . . 55

Tree Farm . . . . . . . . . . . . . . . . 56

When Happiness Is Most Happy . . . . . . . . . 57

Twelve Haiku . . . . . . . . . . . . . . . 58

The Pryers . . . . . . . . . . . . . . . . 61

Sukey and Dr. Glickglick . . . . . . . . . . . . 62

Melanie . . . . . . . . . . . . . . . . . 63

Unto These Least . . . . . . . . . . . . . . 64

Condominium . . . . . . . . . . . . . . . 65

6

Lines Written Beneath An Oak . . . . . . . . . . 66
Brenda's Last Bath . . . . . . . . . . . . . . 67
Monsieur What's-His-Name . . . . . . . . . . . 68
The Intruder . . . . . . . . . . . . . . . 69
I Know, Dear Heart . . . . . . . . . . . . . 70
When, Seeing You Beside Me . . . . . . . . . 71
Clean-Up Day . . . . . . . . . . . . . . . . 72
Cana Re-Visited . . . . . . . . . . . . . . . 73
Terminus . . . . . . . . . . . . . . . . . 74
The Spirit of Man . . . . . . . . . . . . . 75
Déjà Vue . . . . . . . . . . . . . . . . . . 76
The Upward Reach . . . . . . . . . . . . . 77
Winter's Wind . . . . . . . . . . . . . . . 78
Miracle . . . . . . . . . . . . . . . . . 79

# Foreword

SHELDON CHRISTIAN carries forward the American Vision crystalized by Jefferson and Whitman. This vision is of the democratic commonness of all men, creatures, emotions, and things. We all share each other. As Christian says, "There is no place you're not." We, with the grass, are the journey-work of the stars. Here in this book, you are the trapped sparrow, the naval fliers on lonely patrol to Newfoundland; you experience the sudden emotional healing of cleaning an attic; the robust humor of colonial Brunswick, Maine; the effect of sheer panty hose; the spiritual insight into the gigantic forces of the universe.

Never forget that, in the American Vision, nothing is too high or too low to be part of the process. "All the world is God's own field." And the process of sharing each other is a spiritual one. Unless all spirit as well as all matter participate in salvation, there is no salvation for any one.

This is the kind of poetry that you have before you; poetry that can cause you to see and feel that we and everyday things share each other; and this sharing is American in its democracy, and is a holy thing.

RICHARD N. COFFIN

University of Maine, Portland/Gorham

## THE ROAD AGAIN TAKEN

The year of Tom's affair with Mamie Hood,
    Little work got done here on the farm.
I knew the reason; prayed that it would pass;
    And did my best to minimize the harm.

I was not jealous; Mame, I knew, was good;
    And neither sought a lover by design.
What one required, the other had to give;
    And what Tom needed then was hers, not mine.

I yearned to tell him that I understood.
    The road we'd known had vanished in the haze;
But roads abandoned sometimes are resumed:
    How things get done around the place these days!

# THE PEAR TREE

Jane had heard so much about the autumn leaves
That having to stay at home was chief among her peeves.

Others had found the time to drive about the state:
Finally Jim agreed to go, while not too late.

Quickly they raked up the fruit from under the ancient pear,
And dressed up warm because of the nip in the autumn air,

And so they started out, from here to there at will,
Eager for Paradise beyond the next hill.

They went to the locations Jane's friends had raved about,
But there, if once aglow, the fire had now burned out.

There was much of color, fire, and glory still abroad,
But nowhere quite that sense of the radiance of God.

And when Jane told Jim to head for home again,
She questioned, Were these the places her friends had been?

In thoughtful silences, they traversed the final miles,
On their downcast faces, no hint of their usual smiles.

But just as their car turned into their gravel drive,
Both saw the pear tree, and suddenly came alive.

As the setting sun poured its slanting golden light
Into the tree, each leaf shone bright,

Like yellow metal, quivering in the twilight breeze.
It couldn't be real: it must be some kind of magic tease.

"Oh Jim," cried Jane, "here we've been driving far and hard
In search of beauty, only to find it in our back yard!"

## BUMBLEBEE

I remembered having seen a fly
Caught in a spider's web against the sky.
The spider let him waste his waning strength,
Then high-legged it out to pass a length
Of self-spun gut around each wearied wing;
Next she administered a twilight sting,
Then wound the corpus in a gutsy tomb,
And bore her kill back to her dining room.

These thoughts of spider-ways recurred to me
As I looked out and saw a bumble-bee
Crash-land a spider's web with unconcern,
Little suspecting what he soon would learn.
But now I sensed he had become aware
Of the glint-eyed spider lurking in her lair.
You shall not have this bee! I cried. A stick
In hand, I ran to the spot on the double-quick.
With a swipe of the stick I freed the frantic bee,
And saw him freighting off, joyously free.
And I was glad; then asked myself, What made
Me do this? *Could the bumblebee have prayed?*

## MISSION ACCOMPLISHED

The English teacher sought to scratch a spark
Of literary light, but all seemed dark.
"How many've read *The Catcher in the Rye?*"—
He saw no glimmer in some student's eye.
"A friend," the teacher recollected, "saw
Caulfield concentrating in a nook,
And asked what he was reading, hoping to draw
Him into conversation. 'Goddam' book!'
Was Caulfield's bored reply." The teacher then
Observed a paper plane descending from a height:
The sword intrigued them more than did the pen,
And soon a squadron flew in mixed-up flight,
And raucous laughter met his questionings
As still he led their thoughts toward higher things.
At last, the Bell rang; the class withdrew,
Leaving the teacher mentally askew.
He'd given his best, and yet he felt he'd failed:
Their minds flew pilot in these planes they sailed.
A midget plane upon his desk surprised his look,
For neatly lettered on its wings was, "GODDAM' BOOK!"

# THE CAT-BIRD AND THE CATALPA

As I worked, at dusk, in my flower-bed,
I was puzzled by what the cat-bird said,

Then suddenly sensed what the fuss was about:
"Come quickly," he pled, "and help us out!"

And soon, in the gray of the falling night,
I saw what caused the cat-bird's fright.

A tabby-cat with monstrous brow
Was crouching on a catalpa bough.

My bird had lured him from his mate.
Now, seeing me, Old Tab didn't wait:

He turned and bounded down the tree,
As I threw my stone with accuracy.

When I returned to the work I'd begun,
It was now too late to get it done.

But the cat-bird came to where I stood,
And thanked me as plainly as anyone could.

# IN PERPETUUM

### A Cyclus

Into
her heart comes love.
Into her life comes man.
Into her womb comes seed,
the "box in a box"
of man.

Out of
her womb comes child.
Out of her child comes man.
Out of his sac comes seed,
the "box in a box"
of man.

# THE SPARROW TRAP

He had the wash-tub handy, out where the lilacs were.
One dunk of the captured sparrow, and that was the last of her.

The rarer birds were welcome; English sparrows, not.
They devoured seed like locusts, chittered all day, and fought.

The sparrow was, he said (with a few unquotable oaths),
An ill-mannered urchin, with neither song nor clothes.

Experts advised the public, they should be trapped and killed:
One sparrow's chatter now would be forever stilled.

And so he lifted the trap, and was ready to press it down,
And then it would be but moments until the bird would drown.

No longer did she flutter about the cage in fright.
She'd melted into submission, as though accepting her plight.

Indeed was he amazed at the change that took place in the bird.
Her eyes were soft with entreaty; her wing-tip feathers whirred.

It was those pleading eyes that held his gaze engrossed.
She had become a personality, almost.

How could a sparrow's eyes have become so beautiful?
So moist with mute imploring, so completely adorable?—

To such a prayer for mercy, what was there he could say?
He opened up the sparrow trap, and made her fly away.

# THE TRIAL OF GOODWIFE STOVER
### *At Harpswell*

When Goodie Stover passed away
The cry of "witch" swept Casco Bay,

And accusations of her taint
Were vented now without restraint.

"A Freeport Quaker"—this, they knew,
Was why she shunned her Harpswell pew.

Not having lived with godly grace,
Her faith, then, earned no hallowed place.

Cold in her coffin, built of pine,
Her body awaited a word or a sign,

But nary a man would lift a pole
To carry her bier to its graveyard goal.


Six women, at such cowardice,
Picked up the poles, and in a trice,

Began the journey down the road,
Others relieving with the load.

But when they reached the burial ground
They heard a new and dreadful sound:

Discordant voices, pro and con,
The loudest being the devil's spawn.

Ezra Johnson was his name,
And baiting witches was his game.

And now he'd fortified his plea
With a tale of midnight witchery:

In sleep one night, from flesh disjoint,
Imps carried him to Potts's Point.

All over a frigate anchored there,
They dragged him roughly by the hair.

He might have died from bruise and fright
Had not the cock's crow ended night.

And that was when he heard her scream,
"Now let him go!" to her demon team.

He heard her voice transfix the air
As plain as Reverend Eaton's there.

Still deeper hates might have been stirred
Were not the Goodwife's daughter heard

Reminding them in how many ways
Stepmother Stover had eased their days.

Then Goodie Cole, of countless years,
Came to the coffin, and shed salt tears.

What wrongs had Goodie Stover done?—
Each tried, but could not think of one.—

"Take up the bier," aged Eaton said.
"For if she sleeps not with our dead,

No kin of hers need apologize:
That soil is sacred where she lies."

Yet hostile men still blocked the bier.
The women showed no trace of fear

But bore their burden with borrowed strength
Until they reached the graveside's length,

And lowered the box into the space
Reserved for its last resting place.

Then Johnson, like a seven-year-itch,
Persisted, "We have buried a witch!"

But white-locked Eaton, with restraint,
Pronounced, "Good friends, here lies a saint!"

# VAPOR TRAIL

Up there, her whine may tell you, flies a jet,
So high, indeed, you see no silhouette.

In fact, the only sign that gives a clue
May be her vapor trail against the blue.

Moist air, cool-swept by wings, condenses here,
And makes this insubstantial trail appear.

The whitish fleece dissolves as it proceeds,
Two dying lines reborn in twin-purl leads.

Vapor trail! presenting to the ground
At speeds that may approach the flight of sound

A testament that boundless man will fly
To light-far planets in some by and by.

Vapor trail! immensely more than fluff!
Promise of heroic future stuff!

All this, the vapor trail suggests to me,
Of vaster voyagings that yet shall be.

# WHAT HAPPENED AT FAMBRIDGE FERRY
*A Ballad*

Bold Captain Cammock and his love
Urged hard their steed that morning,
Her wrathful father in pursuit
To thwart romance a-borning.

And now at Fambridge Crossing they
Must wait the distant ferry;
The river froths with angry foam,
But Marg'ret prays Tom hurry.

The Earl of Warwick's men draw near
To seize his errant daughter,
So Cammock rowels his seething steed
Into the roiling water.

When they're but half across the tide,
The Earl's great horse starts neighing,
And Cammock struggles to prevent
His own's return, obeying.

At last they climb the farther shore;
At Malden they are wedded;
And seeing that their love is true,
The Earl he blessed them bedded.

# DR. GOSS'S NIGHT OUT

*A Tale of Olde Brunswick*

Time was, when many Brunswickers drank rum
As freely as is coffee now by some.

The potent brew helped pass the lagging hours,
And craftsmen felt that it sustained their powers.

The frames of meeting-houses were raised up
With muscles steeled by access to this cup.

Indeed, the Parson might, thus fortified,
Preach solemnly from Holy Writ, half-pied.

Were things not thus, how could we understand
The fair repute at Dr. Goss' command?

That he was likely crocked was known to all;
But so might be the object of his call.

If he were far from home when darkness fell,
Neighbors would lift him to the saddle; well

His mare knew every road about Maquoit,
And would convey him home with gentle gait.


One day, however, tired of others' ills,
Doc cried, "A pox upon these nastie pills!"

And headed for LaMar's—a kindred soul
Who also bent the elbow at the flowing bowl.

LaMar's privy was within his shed.
Doc saw him leave, and come back comforted.

What Goss didn't guess, was that the sly LaMars
Was out there *putting up the farm-yard bars.*

At last the time arrived for Goss to leave.
The deck was rolling to the ocean's heave;

But the moon was shining with a pretty light,
And Doc could trust his mare to tote him right.

LaMars helped Goss to get the mare re-saddled;
Gave him a hoist; then foxily skedaddled.

Soon the yard was full of wild uproar.
LaMars, in mock amazement at the door,

Saw the shrilling mare go plunging round the yard,
Now charging the fence, now pulled up hard.

"Why, Doc!" he lied, "how come you're still around?
An hour ago, I thought you homeward bound!"

"I was!" roared Goss, unaware of his dripping goad;
"But don't you see? *Some fool has fenced the road!*"

# DOWN EAST

He stood
viewing the
vast Pacific,
quest only begun.
His guides told him,
"Other way,
'Down East'."

He crossed
parched deserts
and great waters.
"I seek Down East-land,"
he cried. Again
they pointed
northeast.

Now, in
fir-tipped Maine,
the east-most state,
they tell him drily,
"Farther down, there
is always
more East."

# THE LYING SOLDIER

There were hardy sons of Erin
  In the War Between the States,
And the greatest were from Maine,
  As my narrative relates.

At the Battle of Antietam
  Patrick fought the Rebs all day,
And was panting from his labors
  When he heard a kinsman say,

"Some one get me to a medic,
  For I fear I'll lose a limb!
Faith, my blood manures this pasture—
  Haste, my sight is growin' dim!"

Patrick quickly caught two horses,
  Set the wounded Gael on one;
Started back to find a sawbones,
  Leadstring making the rear horse run.

But, unknown to Pat, a missile
  Clean de-capped the man thus led.—
Told the soldier's leg was wounded—
  "Leg?" Doc snaps: "he's got no head!"

"Head!" cries Pat; "aint that a caution!
  I'm sure I rightly *heard* the yegg.—
Doc, in such a solemn moment,
  Why'd he lie, and say *his leg?*"

25

## ARGENTIA-BOUND

Night had but fallen when, outside our door,
We heard strange footsteps on the piazza floor.

We thought, at this late hour, who can it be
Here on deserted Harpswell by the sea?

Sheepishly he blinked beneath the ray
Of sudden light. "We've just run out of day.

My friend and I were delivering a boat;
But after dark you do well to stay afloat.

He's busy down there, securing her some more."
(Was this some Flying Dutchman, come ashore?)

"We're flyers," he said, as though he read my mind,
"And must soon leave Brunswick Station behind.

Within three hours, we take off for Argentia."
(Argentia, did he say? or dementia?)

"Our world has shrunk so, you may not understand,"
He said: "Our Naval Base, in Newfoundland."

We fed the flyers, and drove them into town.
They planned to nap, then get their air-gear down.

Fleetly, no doubt, tri-motors in unison,
Their plane soon throbbed above us on her run.

*And do not we find, at the close of life's short day,*
*We still have much to do, in the tasks at which we play?*

*But, before the coming dawn, we too must leave our base,*
*And rise aloft in trust through unfamiliar space,*

*Yet hope, like them, to find, that somehow our Command*
*Will put us safely down in some fair New-Found-Land?*

# THE CHANGING TIDE

As I stood in the night by the ocean,
   And watched the tide go out,
I could see it would not change direction
   In answer to plea or shout.

How long was the tide in recession!
   How long was it lacking in beat!
Before there again came the lapping
   Of little waves at my feet!

And I thought, as I heard the pounding
   Of surf on the low stone wall,
How the tides of man, like the ocean's,
   Are fixed in their rise and fall.

There are tides that wash away fortune,
   Unalterable as fate;
When events in deteriorate motion
   Can counsel us only to wait,

Till at last the ocean's recession,
   Has accomplished its ancient law,
And a new tide is raised by new forces,
   And shoreward begins to draw.

But there's strength to be won from the ocean,
   And this faith from the fathomless sea:
That if one tide can take out one treasure,
   The next may bring new ones to me.

# A GOOD DAY TO GO TO CHURCH

Dark and dismal was the day.
  To find one worse would take research.
A worshiper was heard to say,
  "A good day to go to church!"

But the shadows lifted from the meek,
  And peace infused them, as they bowed;
And when the parson rose to speak,
  The sun broke from behind a cloud.

Of old, he said, the prophets flayed
  The Israelites for bringing in
Defective offerings to be laid
  Upon the Altar for their sin.

And shall we offer to the Lord
  Some less than perfect Sabbath Day?
Shall we then hear His Holy Word
  Only when the sky is gray?

At church, all weathers are the same.
  Here, dewy blessings shower down;
God's Spirit lights our inner flame;
  And heightened health is as our Crown.

Can any day, then, be "too good"
  To spend at church? Our God is there;
And though not all be understood,
  Christ's Joy rewards each patient prayer.

*Come then to church, whatever be the day:*
*And you will meet the Master in the Way.*

# THE COUNTY DAY OF PRAYER

Some months had passed since last they had had rain.
  The springs were dry; the cattle moaned from thirst.
The crops, once lush, were withering away.
  The superstitious feared the County cursed.

That's why a Day of Prayer had been proclaimed
  For public penance, to confess their sin and shame,
And beg the Living God of earth and heaven
  To hear them in the Galilean's name,

And, whatever else, to send them rain—
  The moisture-laden clouds' descending fruit,
To fill the wells and cause the springs to flow,
  Restoring health to herd and flock and root.

Upon the day that had been publicized,
  The people gathered on a sun-parched hill.
The county's most prestigious folk were there,
  To lend the day their presence. Now all were still.

As the Elder lifted up his scrawny arms,
  The people watched. He turned to one who sat
At an organ: "We're ready, Miss Arbella," he said,
  And all then joined in throaty Magnificat.

"My friends," the Elder said, "we're here today
  To confess our sins, and pray to God for rain.
But the Bible tells us, that without faith—FAITH—
  The prayer most desperate is asked in vain.

"And I perceive," he said, "you have no faith."
  The crowd muttered objection, Miss Arbella
Leading their dissent. "It's true!" he cried.
  "We pray for rain: see I *one umbrella*?"

29

## THE DOCTOR'S DICTUM

The symptoms came unheralded,
  Without a reason why;
And what they meant you couldn't be sure,
  Except, you were to die.

You sought your doctor, seeking hope,
  But ready for the truth.
He told you he could promise you
  But one year more of youth.

Half-dazed, you walked the empty streets,
  Not knowing where to turn,
Until surrender brought you peace,
  And faith began to burn.

You did not know when you were healed.
  It left without a trace;
And joyful that you now were well,
  You sought your doctor's place.

But when you stood before his door
  A bordered notice said
He'd see his patients here no more:
  M. Deity was dead.

# BLACK ANGEL

When Job went to bed at his shack that night
There seemed little use in continued fight,
So he moaned to himself as he fell asleep,
"I just can't hack it—I'm in too deep!"
But the sun next morning was shining bright,
    And—tiddie-yi-yeppee, tiddie-yi-yee—
    A cross old crow in the old oak tree
      Croaked, "Up! up! up!"

All Job did next day was to sit and sulk,
So the bigger his troubles seemed to bulk.
"Oh Lord!" he prayed, "I sure need your aid!
So what about the Promise you made?"
But his answer came from the feathered hulk,
    When—tiddie-yi-yeppee, tiddie-yi-yee—
    The cross old crow in the old oak tree
      Croaked, "Up! up! up!"

That night Job studied the starry sea.
"Lord, isn't there help for a bloke like me?
I need a Friend who will show me how.
You don't have an Angel not busy now?"
But when morning came, with sadistic glee
    Still—tiddie-yi-yeppee, tiddie-yi-yee—
    The dour old crow in the old oak tree
      Croaked, "Up! up! up!"

"Aha!" cried Job, "now I understand!
The plain fact is, heaven's undermanned,
So that's why God sends this crow to me,
And he's trying his best to make me see,
You must first help yourself, is His command.
    So—tiddie-yi-yeppee, tiddie-yi-yee—
    That cross old crow in the old oak tree
      Croaks, "Up! up! up!"

# THE FOURTH DIMENSION

The spiritual realm may lie within,
    But yet its reach is wide:
Here present, past, and future meet,
    And places coincide.

All Nature here can be compressed
    Into a single spot:
That spot is you, and yet it's true,
    There is no place you're not.

Within this place we rendezvous
    With those we love or know,
Each traveling as swift as thought—
    Some high, and others low.

Man's faith is in a world of sense—
    Materiality;
And yet this fourth dimension has
    Also Reality.

Our world is full of strange effects
    Not coded by our laws.
This fourth dimension is the realm
    In which they have their cause.

In meditation and in prayer
    We pass its unseen door,
And from this cosmic wonder-world
    God guides us on this shore.

# ATHANASIA

I am as old as time, and shall live until time's end.
No beginning had I, nor to death shall ever bend.
When two stars met, long, long ago,
I was there.
I was in the heat of flame, the flame's red flare.
When the world was being made . . . slow . . . slow . . .
I felt the fight to live, and made my body go.
I was amoeba, fish, amphibian, and man;
All things was I in nature, working out a plan.
Death and life are life alike to me.
When time has cracked, I still shall be.
I am star-dust, muck, and clod.
I am man, and I am God.

# F/LETCHER'S PROGRESS

"Don't fit yourself for a career that will
be obsolete before you graduate,"
young F/letcher's father liked to warn his son.
"That doesn't mean," the Dean would counter-warn,
"you need not study anything at all."[1]
Oh, F/letcher studied; but he most preferred
subjects well-rounded . . . willing . . . yes, and young.
Persistence, charm, and application won
him sweet access to shyly hidden dells.
To these he gave his days as well as nights;
and if his courses were not in the book,
is pussy then less biological?
and when is ardor ever obsolete?
He put into his work all that he had.
*Magna cum laude* weren't excessive praise.
His father could but marvel at such zeal,
and asked for a report in some detail.
The Dean was not the man to tell a lie:
too well he knew techniques for stretching truth.
"Just let me say,"[1] he hedged, with hopes to please,
"that F/lecher[12] gives his best to his stud-ees."[123]

---

[1] With a mild degree of unction, similar to the expression of differing
levels of tonal pitch among certain primitive peoples.
[12] On a higher pitch of ululation.
[123] With an ineffable ecstasy of unctuousness.

## TO REBECCA, WELL SPICED

Rebecca Rand was seldom seen without "Old Spice."
Because the airdale slept with her, she fed him rice.
If you should look Rebecca in the eye, you'd see
The canine looking out at you; and equally

Rebecca looked at you from Spice's hair-crossed brain.
The voice of one had something of the other's strain.
Thus matters stood until the time they clinked their way
Among the customers at Purdy's Shopping Bay.

When they had gone, one woman held her nose and said,
"My God, that dog smelled like he'd eaten something dead."
"That ain't the way," came the reply, "some do the tellin':
What makes you think it was the dog that you was smellin'?"

# WHEN ONE HEAD IS BETTER THAN TWO

One day while on my morning jog
I chanced to meet the weirdest dog.

At sight of him I stared aghast
As The Impossible shambled past:

Close-gripped between his jaws, like bread,
The hound was carrying — his head!

I'd heard of hounds with too much waggage,
But never heads as excess baggage.

But when he moved into the light
I saw my image wasn't right.

His massive head, weighed down by trouble,
Was so low-swung I'd thought it double.

And believe me, friend, when I tell you
One head's to be preferred to two.

And if you don't want folks to say
They saw you with two heads today

While you were walking 'round the town—
Don't let your troubles get you down.

# THE HALF-BAD DOG

*"Give a dog a bad name, and he'll live up to it."*—OLD SAW.

Menander's temper was so violent
    He worried lest his brassy sweetheart would,
If yoked with him, decide his temperament
    Too much for her, and leave him where he stood.

To offset this, he had his friends conspire
    To lie to her, confiding awful things
About him—what a brute he was—his ire;
    But loyally she chose the wedding rings.

Postnuptially, Menander's temper showed.
    He wrecked the bed and chairs; tore the drapes;
And when her parents came, they found the road—
    Assisted through the window by their napes.

Menander next gave undivided thought
    To his espoused. First, he blacked her eyes,
Then gave the room a dusting as they fought,
    Till all resistance melted into cries.

At last she spoke the words he hoped to hear:
    "Your friends told me you go *completely* mad.
I count myself *most fortunate,* my dear,
    To find that you are only *half* so bad!"

## ELEGY TO A LADY-BUG

While at my desk I sit and think
  Of words I wish to say,
A Black Bug makes himself my friend,
  And settles down to stay.

He waddles here, he caroms there,
  With mindless unconcern,
Then mounts the pages of my book
  As though he too must learn.

The Red Bug does not move at all;
  My desk-top once was hers.
She made a charming lady-friend,
  But now no longer stirs.

O Lady-Bug, you've had your day,
  And life for us was sweet;
But now it is the Black Bug's turn,
  So he's the one I'll greet.

## VIEW FROM THE WINDOW-SILL

*An Intimation of Immortality*

Phillipe had set the bird-bath on the ground
    But, hearing Tina tap, looked up in vain.
He knew she stood behind the window-sill,
    Yet all he saw was glistening window-pane.

He thought of that, as now he viewed the scene,
    Looking down from the spot where Tina'd stood,
And noting how, although he moved about,
    The birds behaved as though deep in some wood.

Just so (he mused) might an Invisible be near,
    Observing him, impressing on his mind
High truths not usual for men to hear,
    And only with the Stranger's help divined.

## REMEMBER TO ASK

He was only a junior salesman but
   He had it all down fine,
And it wouldn't be long before he had
   The name upon the line.

But although he had convinced the man
   His product was the best,
The customer merely stood there, with
   The look of a man depressed.

So the salesman started through his stock
   Of arguments again
To be sure he missed no motive that
   Might activate his pen.

"Haven't I proved your old machine
   Too expensive a thing to run?
That it actually costs you money to
   Retain your present one?

Whereas, the moment you begin
   To own this new device,
The tax deduction in itself
   Will prove a profit slice?

Haven't I made these points so clear
   You cannot hesitate
To make up your mind to seize this chance
   To get our Special Rate?"

"You have indeed," the man agreed,
   With a face now quite benign.
"Then in heaven's name, will you explain
   Why it is you do not sign?"

"I'm glad to hear you ask about
   This detail you seemed to forget.
How can I reply, I'll gladly buy —
   When you haven't asked me yet!"

## SNAKE BITE

Well did he know he ought not to pass
At this point into the high grass.
Here, while digging by the road, he'd found
Snakes, and seen their holes in the soft ground.
His gorge rose as they slithered out of sight,
And he would start, as he went to sleep that night.

Now he was spraying gypsy moth nests
Alone the road, and had sprayed most of the pests,
But spied one more in an apple tree,
And forgot that this was where the snakes would be.
It might have been different had he worn
High boots for protection from rock and thorn.

Except for moccasins, his feet were bare;
And down one seam there was a tear.
Happy to think this nest would be the last,
He lunged forward, the sprayer held fast.
The brush in there was dense and hard to take,
And it was then that first he felt the snake.

When its head burst through the broken seam,
His terror was so great he could not scream.
As its cold length now lay beneath his flesh,
He wondered why the reptile did not thresh.
The ancient fear made his quickened heart pound
As he leaped for the road with a frantic bound.

It well could be, the damage had been done
(He thought), and his life's race had now been run.
But first, he would remove the imprisoned snake
From beneath his flesh, and examine for bite or break.
And as he forced his glance down—quick—
He saw the "snake"—a long, green stick.

# CANINE RHAPSODY

Her legs, in stretch-pants, downward stabbed the air;
Her sweater boxed her straight-held shoulders square
As, backward leaning, she clenched tight
The taut leash that pulled her toward the right,
Where something huge sought freedom from her hands,
But got instead her whispered reprimands.
As thus she pranced, opposed to the great hound's pull,
Her breasts, not large, but point-tipped, round, and full,
Rose up and down in rhythm with her walk,
A metronome to her staccato talk.
She high-stepped past. I turned, and found my glance
Ecstatic at the poetry of her pants.
Were I her beast, I'd keep this thought in mind:
Never to lead, but follow her behind.

# THE SEX GODDESS

With what delight I grew aware
Of the Nordic goddess, blonde and fair,
Awaiting her turn in my dentist's chair.

Long legs, sheen-sheathed in panty-hose,
Led up the eye to where arose
A bosom like God-only-knows.

What pleasure it would be to sit
And listen to her cultured wit!
She'd also have a voice to fit.

More beauty still, beneath her dress,
Seemed held in psychical duress.
Had she once been a prophetess?

The dentist crook-armed her inside.
I heard him beg, "Please open wide!"
Time seemed to stop. I all but died!

What words of wisdom might come now
Oracularly from her brow!
And then, she spoke: a peevish, "Ow-w-w-w!"

## BOY CROSSING A FIELD

Pushing hard against the wind,
He hurried down the frost-starred field.
I thought, "This is Monday: strange
That a country lad in Sunday clothes
Should be tearing across a field today."
He changed direction suddenly,
As a boy will with a change of mind.
That was all I saw in that early light,
Except that the hair of the "boy" was white.

# THE UNIVERSAL TONGUE

He'd missed his bird-walks, and the vital sun,
For out-of-doors, he and the birds were one.

No matter what the bird, he knew its speech,
And could communicate in kind with each.

"Good morning," this one sang; "I'm thirsty," that;
And, "Thank you for the food"; or, "H-s-s-t—the cat!"

For weeks, necessity had him at bay,
Researching Gallic authors night and day;

But now, how good it was to take a walk,
And view the birds, and listen to their talk.

But suddenly, he dropped upon a bench,
Amazed, and cried, *"Mon Dieu!* they're talking French!"

# HOW JASON FOUND PARADISE

A pine surmounting Margrave Hill stood stark against the sky,
And Jason thought he'd picture it that day as he drove by.

So, loaded down with photo-gear, he started the ascent,
But soon he saw his effort would most likely be misspent:

The clouds that once had limned the tree were now not to be
    seen;
But still he felt he ought to climb, and view the far marine.

It was, then, not the photograph, that would not let him stop.
He had a mystic sense that he must reach that distant top.

But soon his mind began to reel; he hardly felt his feet;
He asked himself what was the sense enduring all this heat,

Yet felt his torrid climb a thing he was required to do—
As if some Fate had called on him to keep a rendezvous.

At last the steep ascent was won, the goal was there in sight.
He neared the level land that crowned the hill's commanding
    height.

But now the scene that greeted him from crest to sunny bay,
Seemed hardly worth the rugged climb he'd toiled at that hot
    day,

Till just beyond the summit's brow, with timeless modesty,
He saw a girl of ancient grace, one with the sky and sea.

She slowly turned, and gazed at him. He plumbed her ageless
    eyes.
She smiled and said, "We've met at last. My name is Paradise."

# IT WAS NOT SLEEP

It was not sleep; it was not waking still;
It was not day, nor night, nor any time
That ever I have known; nor land nor clime
That I remember—nor plain nor hill.
It was a time of timelessness and void;
A land of landless marks no eye could see;
A wakefulness and sleeping, that neither one might be;
And lacking past and future presently alloyed.
And joy was mine, amid my human fear;
Joy, joy, to sense this timeless unspaced power;
Joy to live eternally within the hour;
Joy to rise beyond the time-swept sphere:
Beloved, in that beyond I never was alone—
Time past, and future-time—always you were my own!

## "HI, MABEL!"

It was a TV "Sidewalk Show"
That pictured the crowd passing to and fro.

The studio staff was prepared for the change of scene,
And the camera was ready to follow Interlocutor Gene.

"It's time," said one, "for that queer little wind-burned runt
To appear suddenly out there and push up front

And wave and smile like a fool at us folks in here.
If he was half attractive, I'd call it a leer."

"Let's ask him, Gene," another staffer said,
"What there is about TV that goes to his head."

"Will do," said Gene, and awaited the sign
From the Show's director that it was exactly nine.

"And you, sir," he said to the little man,
"You like our Show as much as anyone can."

*"Why no, I guess I wouldn't say I do."*
"But why are you always here—can you give us a clue?"

*"I live on the Island. The passage is rough,
And my wife worries I don't row good enough."*

"That's interesting, but let's talk about TV:
Tell us why you're here now, with me."

*"Well, like I said, Mabel—my wife—
Is home worryin' I may have lost my life."*

"Yes, but let's stick to our Sidewalk Show."
*"That's what I mean. That's how she's gonna know."*

"Know what?" *"Know I got across,
No matter how high those waves may toss.*

*She's home, waitin' at her TV;
Tunes into this Channel—and there—*IS ME!

*Hi, Mabel! Water was rough today!
No need to worry! Made it O.K.!"*

48

# THE NESTERS

The painters had gone, and he had just stepped out
To study the job, when he saw the birds about.

The house had been built to get the cooling shade
Cast by the oak that dominated the glade.

There was no mistaking the parental urgency
Impelling the pair to nest in the spreading tree.

But the last thing the man wanted now
Was birds, nesting in some shading bough.

It wasn't the birds themselves that roused his ire:
Their messing was the thing he'd not desire.

And so he watched, and when he'd see them 'light,
He'd shout and wave, and they would take to flight.

He was convinced they must have flown away,
Because he saw them no more after that day.

Autumn came, and the oak tree shed its leaves,
And he was out working under the eaves.

For the first time, as he surveyed his own,
He realized he had not been alone.

Astounded now, he gazed from limb to limb,
And saw what leaves till now concealed from him:

In the crotch of a branch, of verdure now undressed,
There lay exposed the newly-woven nest.

## INDIAN SUMMER

Deep in the forest, his high-cheeked squaw would watch
Their black-eyed papoose, slung from a hemlock bough,
While sewing breeches made from skins of deer.
Another scraped the hairy hide of moose
From which she'd make tough winter moccasins.
The harvest of beans and pumpkin had been good.
Their mat-lined cellars bulged with golden maize.
Soon would the tribe, in graceful white canoes,
Migrate to live off shell-fish on the coast,
Before dispersing for the winter hunt.
There would be plenty for the White Man, too.
So here, beside the waterfall, they met,
The tribal chiefs, to share with him their land.
He drank excessively the White Man's rum,
And felt its madness take control of him.
He passed the White Man water, twig, and turf,
And on his parchment blindly made his mark.
How could he know these men would dam his streams,
Build mills to grind and saw, and frowning forts;
Deplete the wildlife in their greed for furs;
Survey the land, and one day claim it all?

## JOE WEARE, INDIAN FIGHTER

*A Tale of Olde North Yarmouth, Maine*

(*In Colonial days, Indian fighters were called "scouts,"
from the nature of their work.*)

Six feet two of bone and muscle,
Joe had never lost a tussle.

Joe's nickname, "Scout," was his degree,
For he was "full of 'stragedy'."

In childhood Joe would wake up nights
Screaming from dreams of Indian fights.

They'd told him how his Gramp had died:
So hard to kill, the tawnies tried

Twelve times before they'd shot him dead,
Then wound up chopping off his head.

First mounting Granny on a mare,
They tied Gramp's head, dead eyes a-stare,

Beneath her horse's arching neck,
To keep her company to Quebec.

One day, while Yarmouth Joe split rails,
His mind on these and other tales,

A cheerful, chirping chickadee
Was singing from a hemlock tree.

Then six tall tawnies stood around,
As though they'd risen from the ground.

Joe didn't move a single hair.
He "froze"—his sledge still-poised in air.

Then one asked Joe, half through his snout,
"Where live this *sannup*, Joe, the Scout?"

Joe Weare eased down his upraised sledge.
"*Matchet*," said Joe. "Him live on Ledge."

"*Peut-etre* you speak with lying tongue.
You take us to his place among?"

51

Not without reason, as we shall see,
Was Joe called "full of 'stragedy'."

"Would your committee wait a bit,
Till I get this yar timber split?

I'll tellum what you boys can do:
You help me first, then I help you."

One wedge lay deep within a log.
Joe tunked it in, another jog.

Though cracked almost its entire length,
The halves could close with massive strength.

Joe dropped his sledge, so they could see
He stood before them weapon-free.

"You three," said he, "stand over thar—
Like you was standin' at a bar.

You other stinkers—t'other side.
Y'all help me pull this open wide.—

That's great," said Joe. "Now, let's take hold,
And pull like heck when you are told.

First thing you know, we'll have this split,
And I'll have you to thank for it.

Now then," said Joe, plain full of bull,
"Wait till I strike, and then—*you pull.*"

But when he struck, the crafty Scout
Knocked *up* the wedge, so it sprang *out!*

The half-clove log snapped shut again,
And gripped the hands of all six men,

And strain and tug as each one might,
He found both hands were locked in tight.


Then Joe took up his trusty axe.
"You can shout till they hear you in Halifax,

But you're dealin' with me now—Joe, the Scout,
And we got business to talk about.

I'm sure my Gran'paw Up There sends
His hopes you all meet fittin' ends."

And with each taunt, he swung the blade,
Collecting interest on that raid,

Till each received the *coup de grace,*
And joined his ancestors *en masse.*


Joe Weare "the Scout" deserved the name:
Outsmarting smarties was his game.

Those wars are over; now there's peace;
But Joe Weare's fame will never cease.

# GENTLEMEN WEAR JACKETS

These modern Magi of the sciences,
Though natives once to many ancient tongues,
Conversed in English at this posh resort,
And shared their findings as their forebears had;
Not as humanists, but scientists the more.
One boasted, The bomb that razed Hiroshima
Had served them well to wake a sleeping world,
And what was needed now, was a bigger one,
Dropped each decennium or so
On some too somnolent metropolis . . . .
I heard not one reproach or least dissent.
It was, of course, what you might call *their bomb*.
They were entitled to their sense of pride
In this fantastic engine they had made;
But when I said that priests of other cults
Questioned how much more of this our world
Can take, they closed their minds and cast me out.
As then we chattered to the banquet hall,
I read a placard, ruling, "Gentlemen
*Must* wear jackets in the dining room."

*Problem: find Lady Debra.*

## LADY DEBRA
### *A Limerick*

*(Suggested by hearing a British Colombian on an African Safari speak of what he called a "Zeb-bra.")*

A horsy young damsel named *Deb*-bra,
Would, unclothed, ride bareback a *zeb*-bra.
   So they painted her stripéd —
   Blent quadru- with biped—
Till a "vet" cou'n't detect her ver*teb*-bra.

Our Zebra illustration, by Thomas Bewick, has been reproduced from Ralph Beilby's *A General History of Quadrupeds*, London, 1790, through the courtesy of the Bowdoin College Library Special Collections.

# TREE FARM

The couple looked like forty-four;
  We knew that they were older.
Their children helped them run the farm,
  In summery days and colder.

Now Trenton there, a handsome youth,
  Was ready to be married.
We asked them all about the lad,
  And so they talked and tarried.

"The day we take down one tree here
  We plan to plant another.
That's been our rule on this old farm—
  There won't be any other.

"Right there once stood a handsome birch,
  As fine as you could fancy,
But we required the site to build
  That house for Ned and Nancy.

"Each cut we made was like a wound
  Upon ourselves inflicted;
The sap that flowed was like the blood
  Our inner hurts evicted.

"And when at last the trunk lay low
  We heard unspoke a sentence,
That bid us purge ourselves of sin
  By Nature's prime repentance.

"That law is clear: we must replace
  Each tree that we have taken,
Restoring nature's balance thus
  Whenever it is shaken.

"That afternoon we bathed and slept,
  Then rendered unto nature
That which was due her for the life
  We'd taken of such stature.

"And deep within ovarian soil
  The seed was germinating,
And Trenton was our tree that day,
  According to our dating."

## WHEN HAPPINESS IS MOST HAPPY

Happiness is
    not only the warmth of the sun's shining,
    not only the affection of friends and lovers,
    not only the recognition of hard-won success.

      These are emotional high-rises on
        the level landscape of the new day,
      But they are happinesses that have their rise
        without.

Happiness also is
    the warmth you feel from the shining of the inner sun,
    the affection you feel flow out to seek other's embraces,
    the joy you feel when, knowing
      that though others may not yet understand
      the quality of your good work,
    you do; and contemplating it,
      toward the end of your small day of creativity,
        you feel the work is good.

Happiness is most happy
        when it has its rise
           within.

## J.F.K.
He will never grow old.
The ages will know him young.
Not for him, Death.


## NOW
The hottest flame cools;
The longest years are numbered:
Wait not, then, to live.


## CELEBRATION
The nesting swallow
Crazily flits to and fro—
Handing out cigars.


## IVY
Reach still for the Rock.
Can'st thou not cling, thou'lt wither:
Clinging gives thee Life.

## ECOLOGY

A lean ant drags off
The fat fly I just swatted.
Nothing goes to waste.

## TACT

Shooing the bold fly,
The wise take care not to break
The treasured China.

## THE IMPOSSIBLE

Flight dynamics prove
The thing's not possible; yet
The bumblebee flies.

## FATAL GUEST

Under the rose leaf
The caterpillar fattens,
Consuming its host.

## THE FALL

Earth's snow-white bedspread
Conceals winter's dark secret:
Virgin Spring's pregnant.


## RESURRECTION

Disdained, the spilled seed,
Embalmed in ice, will yet rise
To adore the sun.


## RIP VAN WRINKLES

Waking from his nap,
What astounded him was, how
All his friends had aged.

## THE PRYERS

Peeping through his binocs
  At the Maine woods shack,
He sees within, a pryer
  Likewise peeping back.

# SUKEY AND DOCTOR GLICKGLICK

This was one on Doctor Glickglick:
Sukey phoned him she was sick-sick,
Wanted him to hurry quick-quick.
Sukey's voice was very thick-thick.

"I'll be there in Time's li'l nick-nick,"
Doc said; but first he used his Schick-Schick,
Then smoothed his face with creamy ick-ick,
Drank some milk till he went hic-hic,

Turned down his oil-lamp's flaming wick-wick,
Shook his watch till it went tick-tick,
Grabbed his trusty walking stick-stick,
Booted closed his door with a kick-kick,

Wrote a note with his faithful bic-bic,
Climbed aboard his Moby Dick-Dick,
Slithered off to Sukey's, slick-slick,
Like no problem he couldn't lick-lick.

*"I'm O.K., now, Doctor Glickglick,"*
*Sukey smiled. "You didn't come quick-quick."*

# MELANIE

### 1

Perhaps it was because I sometimes see
Fresh mystery in little ones that I
That day fell quite in love with Melanie,
A dark-eyed child at play as I passed by.
Her mother came to see my wife, not me;
And while the queen was made a butterfly,
Her father crawled inside a hive of news,
And Melanie skipped rope with whisking shoes.

### 2

I must confess I tried to flirt with her
(If you could call benignant smiling this).
She turned away, her rope a pervious blur.
But Dante won a smile from Beatrice,
A touch that made his whole life rosier.
Still, I concede, a look can plant a kiss,
So Melanie was wise to be unnerved,
And I got what I probably deserved.

### 3

Only too soon the queen came buzzing back,
The radio's drone was silenced, Melanie
And mother legged it inside, and like a hack
The car departed, stiff and crochety.
"You keep your eyes to home," it seemed to clack.
But I surprised the child, anxiously
Searching for me from the leaving bus,
Eyes large as plums, and luminous.

## UNTO THESE LEAST

The woman doctor, through the window pane,
Could see the bird preparing to remain.

"You'd better hurry, little one, and go-it,
Or a snow-storm will be here before you know it."

The little bird seemed strangely unafraid.
Crouching in the station, there she stayed.

It was the doctor's duty to telephone
A patient's survivors. In anesthetic tone

She told how gently Death had come, in sleep;
So gently, their loved one would not have them weep.

Concluding on this reassuring word,
She turned to the window, to see about the bird.

She knocked on the pane; the bird declined to stir.
So out the doctor went to look at her.

But now, in frenzy, she is back again,
Holding in her hands the tiny wren,

A child who can not now be comforted,
Crying, "The precious little dear is—dead!"

# CONDOMINIUM*

So we were back in the land of pointed fir,
Glad to escape the city's smells and sounds.
Motionless, I sat and faced the sea,
Proud as I surveyed the well-kept scene,
For on these eastland acres I was lord,
With sovereign title to this much of earth.

I watched a mole creep out to nibble grass;
A prankster of a chipmunk reared himself
Half from his hole to stare round-eyed at me;
Except the circling, raucous-mewing gulls,
A dozen birds were calling joyously;
A lanky crane stood like a unipod,
While, in a distant meadow, deer browsed.
I saw now, that when we were not there
My property was not untenanted.
That it was mine alone was not, then, true:
The only difference was, I paid the taxes.

*Literally, shared lordship. —*Dict.*

# LINES WRITTEN BENEATH AN OAK

What are the words that your branches say
As I rest from the heat of the summer's day?
What are the tales I am sure you could tell
Were it not that your lips have been sealed so well?

Doubtless you'd speak of a passionate tryst —
Or perhaps of the dawn and its slow-moving mist —
Of thunder, and lighting, and sunshine again,
Or the whiteness of winter while snowfalls remain.

Solemnly skyward you rear your great length,
As you thrill to the knowledge of uncommon strength —
Strength that is more than enough for your need,
That mothers the wood-folk and shadows the seed.

Through the years you have struggled and learned to endure;
You've suffered and prayed and are noble and pure.
As you wordlessly reach your great arms to the sky,
I sense you have spirit as well as have I.

## BRENDA'S LAST BATH

My Brenda loved to linger at her bath,
So this was not the time to cross her path.

Besides, the bathroom reeked with exotic scents,
And errant soaps inviting accidents.

That this immersion benefited her,
Her voice revealed in rising caliber.

But suddenly these sounds were heard no more . . .
Concerned, I went and peeked in through the door,

And then rushed in, I'm sure with frantic air,
At seeing now no sign of Brenda there;

Then realized at last why search for her was vain:
She'd pulled the plug too soon, and gurgled down the drain.

## MONSIEUR WHAT'S-HIS-NAME

Adrien Le Couvreur was a lover tabbed by Destiny.
He'd waited half his life for a beauty like Mimi.

His was a total love — and hopeless, as one might say —
Which bound him fast forever, beginning that fatal day,

For unfortunately the *femme* whose favor he hoped to win
Had no intention of being either wife or mistress to him.

So he put his affairs in order, then shot himself in the head,
And his servants found him lying — in blood, and cold, and dead.

There were those who suspected his secret, and told it to Mimi.
Her *toilette* was *toute fini*. She was ravishing to see.

"What a pity!" she absently murmured, "for love to make such
a stir. —
I don't remember the man. Did you say his name was *Bonheur?*"

# THE INTRUDER

I had entered the gates of a Lombardy town,
  And with hand on my sword strolled the street that night
When, near to a house of ancient reknown,
  My blood all but froze at a scream filled with fright.

I leaped to the casement to peer inside,
  And pushed back the drapes that clung to my head,
Then feared for myself at what I descried,
  For a murder was taking place on the bed.

A brute of a man had his teeth at the throat
  Of a lady he handled most shoddily,
And though she was gripping both ears of the goat,
  Her assailant had mounted her bodily.

I caught glimpses of flesh moist-beaded with sweat,
  And of scratches still bleeding where nails had incised.
With the life and death struggle undecided as yet,
  I heard her impassioned appeal to her Christ.

"Lady," I ventured, "suffer you pain?"
  (This violence I was vexed t' see.)
"Aye, sire," she cried, "but not in vain:
  It's the agony of ecstasy."

# I KNOW, DEAR HEART

I know, dear heart, there have been trying times
When it has seemed our love has flown away;
When we have known the dull and cheerless day
As well as those that echoed marriage chimes.

I know, dear heart, how hard it must have been
When, tossed about by business cares,
I proved no easy field to weed of tares,
And you could little know what nor when.

And well I know, dear heart, how oft you've done
The thing you thought would please me most, and yet
Have found me as distressed as I could get,
And peace and settled love seemed never won.

And yet, perhaps, my love, it is these little things
That are our lasting bonds and daily-given rings.

## WHEN, SEEING YOU BESIDE ME

When, seeing you beside me, fast asleep,
Your face reposed, with cheer upon your cheek,
Your breath slow-coming, and your mouth set meek,
And knowing you my own to love and keep;

When, next the blazing hearth we crouch,
And sip the morning coffee from the cup,
And, slow to wake, delay our rising up,
And feel regret to leave so soon our couch;

When, through the day, we tell the fulsome news
That from our lives the time has brought to each,
And seek the lesson that the news may teach,
Yet feel continued Love is greater news —

In these moments, Love, my heart, though glad,
Grows cold for fear good news some time turn bad.

# CLEAN-UP DAY

All day we labored in the dusty barn
To clear its loft of things of yesterday,
So long too dear to even give away,
Since that telegram about the Marne.
That joint-loose high chair; childhood magazines;
Those battle toys once strewn about the floor;
Those well-worn clothes our boy would wear no more;
These souvenirs of teen-age birthday scenes—

All these had held us past-bound to this place.
That some day, all of them must go, we'd known;
Yet this farewell was more than we could face.
But now the time had come. We both had grown.
With love for every moment of the past,
We cleared the loft, and both stood healed at last.

## CANA REVISITED

The young god's mother came to him and said,
"They have no wine," and he reluctantly
Bid then the servants fill the jars of stone.
They poured in water; they drew out wine,
So choice, indeed, the master of the feast
Said to the Bridegroom, "The usual practice is,
To serve the good wine first, till the guests are drunk;
But you have saved the choicest wine for last."

And you, my love, whom, in youth's sweet flush,
Invoking Cana's memories, I wed,
Have drunk with me life's wines and found them good,
Till I had feared our Joy might be used up;
But now, from jars fresh-filled, you serve me wine
That makes our latter love a cup divine.

*John* 2:1-12.

# TERMINUS

Orlando's office now was in his home.
He liked the ease of going off to work
By simply entering the added room,
And changing then into The Company.
One thing, however, he'd not counted on:
His wife began to dog him while at work,
As though each hour had special preciousness.
He did not understand, and closed his door.
But then he'd fume within his fiscal fort,
Not able still to free himself of her.
He knew her out there haunting to come in,
Projecting a plea she could not verbalize.
One day he realized this was no woman's whim:
Her time was running out. He took her in with him.

# THE SPIRIT OF MAN

Who best exemplifies the Spirit of Man? the Priest?
   Not all who are in holy orders
   Are priests and priestesses:
      Not all who are priests and priestesses
      Are in holy orders.
To be a priest, though not in holy orders,
Is greater than to be ordained by any Church:
For the objective of the Church should be free people.

Who best exemplifies the Spirit of Man? the Parent?
   Not all who have borne children
   Are fathers and mothers:
      Not all who are fathers and mothers
      Have borne children.
To be a father or a mother, though childless,
Is greater than to have given birth to many,
Because parental love is maximized in love for all.

Who best exemplifies the Spirit of Man? the Teacher?
   Not all who teach
   Have learned life's basic lessons:
      Not all who have learned life's basic lessons
      Seek to give instruction.
To have learned, and then to exemplify the lesson,
Is the highest teaching,
Because what we really teach is what we are.

Who best exemplifies the Spirit of Man? the Physician?
   Not all physicians are imbued with healing Power:
   Not all who have that Power are physicians.
To be a healer is to help to wholeness any who hunger
      to become more whole.
He best exemplifies the Spirit of Man who acts from love.
The Spirit of Man, therefore, is of God: for God is love.

# DÉJÀ VUE
## By Sheldon Christian

My beloved speaks to me—words I have heard before.
I answer her with words that come from another shore.

Does she somehow feel as I do, incarnate with mystic lore,
That everything we do here, we have done before?

Haven't we walked, as now, this very woodland path?
Didn't I then, when angered, strike her in my wrath?

And didn't I lift and hold her mutely crumpled form,
And press her closer still, after my temper's storm?

   (All this I'd done in eons gone,
    And loved this self-same woman long.)

But now, I seem to open a new and different door.
This time, I've mastered my temper, and have not let it roar.

This time, I did not strike her, as once I did before.
For now I have stilled the tempest, and become its conqueror.

# THE UPWARD REACH

My son would look at me, his eyes
    Seeing, not his mind;
But on that day, he looked at me
    And recognized his kind.

I saw perception strike the spark
    That made him self-aware,
And in that moment he was Man,
    With self-consciousness to share.

Each day we strive for higher birth
    Above the common Man,
And seek to tune our higher selves
    To blend with cosmic Plan.

Tomorrow we'll know fuller Love,
    And psychic powers, too;
And we will learn much more of Truth
    Than now we trust is true.

O Love, that lights all hallowed hearts,
    O Tears, that cleanse all eyes:
Shine now within, lave clear our sight —
    Assist our souls' uprise.

# WINTER'S WIND

In silhouette, the leaf-lorn branches of these oaks
Flail as this late-autumn storm renews its strokes.

The foaming waves break upon the rock-strewn beach,
Glistening with hoar-frost as far as eye can reach.

How bare the landscape seems, and barer still to be.
The drifted leaves compact themselves for surety.

Ah, my friend-trees, chilled by this wintry blast —
To others also changes come, and, too, come fast.

The breath of winter strips the leaves from other trees —
For through my life has also blown a gelid breeze.

The love of spring that bore your fluttering green
Was mine, too; and not soon will there again be seen

The leafy body given life by summer's sun.
But we can only take our seasons one by one;

And I'm not that unhappy, really, my dear trees.
Winter is a time of bended boughs — and knees;

And that which bends can be made strong by doing so:
We'll welcome winter's wind — and let it help us grow.

## MIRACLE

When I was young, and all credulity,
Life was full of endless mystery.

My middle years were years of woe.
I saw my fairy fancies go.

From month to month, up through the years,
I had no wish for laughter or for tears.

The past few months have brought a change.
My life is feeling all the range

Of joy and sorrow, and the wonderment
That all the mysteries of old had lent.

Old tales again are beautiful and sweet,
For I have bound the shoes of childhood on my feet.

## BY THE SAME AUTHOR

THIRTY YEARS OF TUFTS VERSE
*An Anthology,* 1931

POEMS ABOUT MAINE
*An Anthology,* 1940

*Brochures*

125 YEARS OF RELIGIOUS PIONEERING
*A Parish History,* 1937

THE UNBEAUTIFUL SPEAR
*Foreword by* John Haynes Holmes
*A Poem,* 1937

OUR BLESSED LADY'S TUMBLER
*A One Act Play,* 1948